For:_____

*Y*ou have made known
to me the path of life.

❧

—*Psalm 16:11*

From:_____

Mom, I Love You!
Copyright 1999 by ZondervanPublishingHouse
ISBN 0-310-97815-7

Requests for information should be addressed to:

ZondervanPublishingHouse
Mail Drop B20
Grand Rapids, Michigan 49530
http://www.zondervan.com

Senior Editor: Gwen Ellis
Project Editor: Pat Matuszak
Design: Chris Gannon
Printed in China
> 99 00 01 02 / HK/ 4 3 2 1

Mom,
I Love You!

ZondervanGifts

We have a gift for inspiration™

Mom
I Love You!

Love one another deeply,
from the heart.

≈

—1 Peter 1:22

Mom
I Love You!

$\mathcal{K}$ids are like sponges: they
absorb all your strength and leave
you limp; but give 'em a squeeze
and you get it all back!

—*Barbara Johnson*

Mom
I Love You!

She watches over the affairs of
her household. . . .
Her children arise and call her
blessed.

❧

—Proverbs 31:27–28

6

Mom

I Love You!

*M*y children usually arise and call me, "Ma!" I wonder, does anyone know that my real name is twice as long as the one I'm usually called?

—*Jean Syswerda*

Mom
I Love You!

$\mathcal{M}$ay your unfailing love be
my comfort, O LORD.

❦

—*Psalm 119:76*

Mom

I Love You!

$\mathcal{T}$he Lord is sure to accomplish
those things a loving heart has
waited long to see.

❧

—*Bessie Porter*

Mom
I Love You!

*T*he LORD will yet fill your
mouth with laughter
and your lips with shouts of joy.

—*Job 8:21*

Mom
I Love You!

*L*aughter cloaks itself in disguise
and springs out from its hiding
place to surprise us—it shouts,
Olly, Olly, oxen free! It invites us
to rush to life's game again.

—*Karen Burton Mains*

Mom

I Love You!

$\mathcal{F}$ind rest, O my soul, in God alone;
my hope comes from him.

—*Psalm 62:5*

12

Mom
I Love You!

$\mathcal{B}$y and large, mothers and
housewives are the only
workers who do not have
regular time off. They are
the great vacationless class.

❧

—*Anne Morrow Lindberg*

13

Mom
I Love You!

God's compassions never fail.
They are new every morning.

❧

—Lamentations 3:22–23

Mom

I Love You!

$\mathcal{I}$f I could, I'd write for you a rainbow
And splash it with all the colors of God
And hang it in the window of your being

❧

—*Ann Weems*

*C*hildren's children are a crown . . .
and parents are the pride of their children.

—*Proverbs 17:6*

Mom
I Love You!

$\mathcal{I}$ will never forget the day my first grandchild, Lindsay, was born. What a happy time! After all the years of raising my own children with all the struggles, I could now see the fruits of my labors. It was as though life's cycle was completed.

—Nancy Corbett Cole

*T*hose who hope in the LORD will
renew their strength.
They will soar on wings like eagles.

—Isaiah 40:31

Mom
I Love You!

$\mathcal{O}$ur souls were made to "soar on wings" and they can never be satisfied with anything short of flying.

—*Hannah Whitall Smith*

Mom
I Love You!

$\mathcal{I}$ will turn darkness into light
before them
and make the rough places
smooth.

❧

—*Isaiah 42:16*

Mom
I Love You!

$\mathcal{L}$earn to set aside what you see
and hear in order to see and hear
what God would pour out upon
you from his invisible kingdom.

—*Saint Theresa of Avila*

Mom
I Love You!

See, I am doing a new
    thing! . . .
I am making a way in the
    desert.

—*Isaiah 43:19*

Mom
I Love You!

*W*hat a privilege God has
given us to love one another!

—*Susan Lenzkes*

Mom
I Love You!

Keep on loving each other.

—*Hebrews 13:1*

Mom

I Love You!

$\mathcal{A}$s a mother I was obligated to meet my daughter's needs. But what a joy it was when I could delight her heart by giving her some of the fun stuff too— surprises, extras—just for pure pleasure.

—*Carole Mayhall*

Mom
I Love You!

$\mathcal{I}$ will make an everlasting
covenant with you,
my faithful love promised to
David.

❧

—Isaiah 55:3

Mom
I Love You!

$\mathcal{B}$ehind every prayer and behind
every promise, there is God.

—*Hannah Whitall Smith*

Mom
I Love You!

$\mathcal{W}$ho trusts in the L<small>ORD</small> . . .
    will be like a tree planted by
    the water
    that sends out its roots by the
    stream.

           ❧

      —Jeremiah 17:7–8

Mom

I Love You!

$\mathcal{H}$elp me to give my children good roots, God. Enriched with good music, good books, good talk, good taste. But above all, goodness of spirit. Goodness of action.

—Majorie Holmes

Mom
I Love You!

"*Y*our work will be rewarded,"
declares the LORD. . . .
"Your children will return to their
own land."

❧

—*Jeremiah 31:16–17*

Mom
I Love You!

$\mathcal{L}$ord, I want to see each of my
children belong wholly to you.

—*Shirley Pope Waite*

Mom
I Love You!

*J*esus said, "Let the little children come to me, and do not hinder them, for the kingdom of heaven belongs to such as these."

—*Matthew 19:14*

Mom
I Love You!

*T*he story of Christ blessing the
children is not only for the nursery
but for adults as well. If he could
welcome the interruption of his
ministry by wiggling, wonderstruck
humanity, can we dare do less?

—*Karen Burton Mains*

Mom *I Love You!*

$\mathcal{T}$rust in the LORD at all times . . .
pour out your hearts to him.

❧

—Psalm 62:8

Mom
I Love You!

$\mathcal{D}$ear Lord, I want this little boy to know how much I love him. Help me to show him how much by the sparkle of delight in my eye when I smile, by how quick I am to drop a mother's chores and play, by the unhurried way I read stories—even those I've read a hundred times before.

✌

—*Mary C. Wells and Judy Gire*

Mom
I Love You!

$\mathcal{W}$e have put our hope
in the living God.

❧

—*1 Timothy 4:10*

Mom
I Love You!

F attribute my discovery of my
heavenly Father largely to my
earthly parents. Not by talking, but
by daily living, were impressions
made on our childish hearts.

❧

—*Hannah Whitall Smith*

Mom
I Love You!

$\mathscr{B}$e rich in good deeds . . . take
hold of the life that is truly life.

❧

—1 Timothy 6:18–19

Mom
I Love You!

$\mathcal{I}$ have learned from a good friend, a woman my mother's age. For some wonderful, unknown reason, God must have put me "in her basket." She made me feel that I'd be doing her a favor by accepting her deeds of love.

❧

—*Colleen Townsend Evans*

BERTHA

39

Mom
I Love You!

Your hands made me and
formed me.

❦

—*Psalm 119:73*

Mom

I Love You!

I love it when my children bring
their artwork to me. Their proud
smiles tell me how they feel.
"What a wonderful drawing!"
I say. "Let me hang it on the fridge
where everyone can enjoy it."

❧

—*Cynthia Culp Allen*

41

Mom
I Love You!

*L*ook to the heavens:
Who created all these?
He who brings out the starry host one by one,
and calls them each by name.
Because of his great power and mighty strength,
not one of them is missing.

⁂

—*Isaiah 40:26*

Little Zoe, our granddaughter, was coming home with us. She looked up through the windshield at a sky studded with stars. "I wonder how God keeps the stars up there," she said. "Do you think he uses white glue?"

—*Zoe B. Metzger*

43

Mom
I Love You!

$\mathcal{T}$he LORD makes me lie down
in green pastures,
he leads me beside quiet waters,
he restores my soul.

—Psalm 23:2–3

Mom

I Love You!

*M*ost evenings I spend a few
minutes at the door looking over
my backyard. The holy hush of
my wooded backyard is my
cathedral. The wind whispers
to me of a God who is there.

❧

—*Jean E. Syswerda*

Mom
I Love You!

$\mathcal{T}$he LORD has done great things
for us,
and we are filled with joy.

❧

—*Psalm 126:3*

Mom
I Love You!

*J*oy is a net of love by which
you can catch souls. One gives
the most who gives with joy.

❧

—*Mother Teresa of Calcutta*

Mom
I Love You!

$\mathcal{W}$hoever claims to live in him must walk as Jesus did.

❧

—*1 John 2:6*

Mom

I Love You!

$\mathcal{I}$m taking a lifetime class in the art of being Christlike. As he teaches me, I try to imitate him. Studying his Word helps me. Jesus painted the whole New Testament with a broad sweep of love, forgiveness and mercy.

—*Cynthia Culp Allen*

Mom
I Love You!

Encourage one another
and build each other up.

❧

—1 Thessalonians 5:11

Mom
I Love You!

$\mathcal{E}$ncouragement gives us the
strength to do what we feel
we cannot do, hold on when we
feel we cannot hold on, and try
what we might not dare.

❧

—*Sharon Mahoe*

Mom
I Love You!

$\mathcal{F}$ will give them singleness of heart
and action . . . for their own good and
the good of their children after them.
I will make an everlasting covenant
with them: I will never stop doing
good to them, and I will inspire them.

❧

—Jeremiah 32:39–40

Mom
I Love You!

*H*elp me achieve a firm and
steadfast faith in the Lord Jesus
that will enable me to manage
the common affairs of life.

❧

—*Prayer of Susanna Wesley*

Mom
I Love You!

We are God's workmanship.

—Ephesians 2:10

Mom
I Love You!

$\mathcal{I}$ think back over the last few
years and wonder at the grace
and kindness of God to me. . . .
Now I find myself the home for
this precious gift from God.

❦

—*Sheila Walsh, awaiting the birth of her child*

Mom

I Love You!

$\mathcal{F}$or God so loved the world that
he gave his one and only Son,
that whoever believes in him shall
not perish but have eternal life.

—*John 3:16*

Mom

I Love You!

$\mathcal{A}$t the end of our life, we
shall be judged by love.

—*St. John of the Cross*

Mom
I Love You!

$\mathscr{W}$here your treasure is, there
your heart will be also.

—*Matthew 6:21*

Mom

I Love You!

$\mathcal{M}$other's arms wrap me in
warmth, and I am home. A
forty-year-old child reassured
by her mother's touch. There
is no time in touch.

❦

—*Ruth Senter*

Mom
I Love You!

$\mathcal{L}$ORD, you establish peace for us.

❧

—Isaiah 26:12

Mom
I Love You!

Only parents' love
can last our lives.

❧

—*Robert Browning*

Mom
I Love You!

Clothe yourselves with compassion, kindness, humility, gentleness and patience. Bear with each other.

—Colossians 3:12–13

Mom
I Love You!

$\mathcal{I}$ am convinced that God's
Holy Spirit orchestrates
our lives to touch others.

—*Becky Tirabassi*

If any of you lacks wisdom . . . ask God, who gives generously to all.

—James 1:5

Mom
I Love You!

$\mathcal{I}$t is God who guides us into truth and who reveals his truth in his Son Jesus and in his Word.

❦

—*Catherine DeVries*

*J*esus said to her, "I am the
resurrection and the life."

❧

—*John 11:25*

Mom
I Love You!

$\mathcal{T}$o speak of God as the
"living God" is to make the
claim that God is actively
present, here and now.

❧

—*Rebecca Manley Pippert*

Mom
I Love You!

"For I know the plans I have
for you," declares the
LORD, "... plans to give
you hope and a future."

❧

—*Jeremiah 29:11*

Mom
I Love You!

$\mathcal{H}$ere on earth, you live by faith.
In heaven, you will understand
it all and thank God for his
wisdom in every little thing.

❧

—*Kay Marshall Strom*

Mom
I Love You!

So then, just as you
received Christ Jesus
as Lord, continue
to live in him.

※

—*Colossians 2:6*

Mom

I Love You!

*T*his is the mystery we were made
to contain: the very life of Jesus.
We are the glove; he is the hand.
We are the cup; he is the coffee.
We are the lamp; he is the light.

—*Claire Cloninger*

71

Mom
I Love You!

$\mathcal{F}$ have set the LORD always
    before me.
Because he is at my right hand,
    I will not be shaken.

❦

—Psalm 16:8

Mom
I Love You!

Christ who surrounds you—above
you, beneath you, around you, before
you, behind you, within you. This is
the Christ who is all, and in all. You
are complete, "running over," in him!

—Anne Ortlund

Mom
I Love You!

$\mathcal{E}$ncourage one another daily,
as long as it is called Today.

—Hebrews 3:13

Mom
I Love You!

$\mathcal{T}$he "future is now" means
you are seated in the presence
of God. Knowing that each
moment is the Lord's, frees us
from seeing all of life as work.

—*Carol Van Klompenburg*

I will praise the LORD, who
counsels me;
even at night my heart
instructs me.

—Psalm 16:7

Mom

I Love You!

My "house" is placed into the
loving arms of Jesus; I rest in
him and sleep without fear.

—*Alice C. Peter*

Mom
I Love You!

Jesus said to the waves, "Quiet!
Be still!" Then the wind died
down and it was completely calm.

❦

—*Mark 4:39*

Mom
I Love You!

$\mathcal{T}$he gift of peace can come quietly,
unexpectedly—as you gaze at the
soft glow of a candle during a hushed
quiet time—through the loving
gesture of a friend—through laughter
or tears or simply silence.

—Betsy Lee

A word aptly spoken
is like apples of gold in
settings of silver.

❦

—*Proverbs 25:11*

Mom
I Love You!

A hundred years from now it will
not matter what my bank account
was, the sort of house I lived in, or
the kind of car I drove . . . but the
world may be different because I was
important in the life of a child.

—*Anonymous*

81

Mom
I Love You!

She gets up while it is still dark;
    she provides food for her family.

—*Proverbs 31:15*

Mom
I Love You!

*T*here is no giver like a mom. She stays up late and gets up early to see that all the loose ends are tied up for tomorrow. She learns to remember what each child is most likely to forget and runs an endless taxi and delivery service. And she just keeps on giving.

—*Pat Matuszak*

*M*ay the words of my mouth
    and the meditation of my heart
be pleasing in your sight,
O LORD, my Rock and my
Redeemer.

❧

—Psalm 19:14

84

Mom
I Love You!

*J*ust because we are there, day
in and day out, we may
throw the balance toward our
children's lifetime stability.

❧

—*Kate Convissor*

Mom

I Love You!

The Lord will be your confidence.

—*Proverbs 3:26*

Mom
I Love You!

$\mathcal{W}$e are created to shine with the light of God's creative genius. When you appreciate yourself in all your uniqueness, you will dare to live out the beauty you were created to express, cleaned and polished with the forgiveness of God.

❧

—*Connie Neal*

Mom

I Love You!

$\mathcal{T}$he kingdom of heaven is like
treasure hidden in a field.

—*Matthew 13:44*

Mom

I Love You!

$\mathcal{L}$ife is not always what one wants it to be, but to make the best of it, as it is, is the only way of being happy.

—*Jennie Jerome Churchill (Winston Churchill's mother)*

Mom
I Love You!

$\mathcal{I}$ am the vine; you
are the branches.

—*John 15:5*

Mom
I Love You!

$\mathcal{P}$rayer means launching out of the heart toward God; a cry of grateful love from the crest of joy or the trough of despair: it is a vast, supernatural force that opens my heart, and binds me close to Jesus.

—*Saint Therese of Lisieux*

Mom

I Love You!

For you make me glad by your deeds,
O LORD;
I sing for joy at the works of your
hands.
How great are your works, O LORD,
how profound your thoughts!

❧

—*Psalm 92:4–5*

Mom
I Love You!

$\mathcal{B}$ecause I know myself
accepted and loved by Christ,
I am able to accept myself
fully and to say with my whole
heart, "I enjoy being a woman."

—*Ingrid Trobisch*

Mom
I Love You!

$\mathcal{W}$hatever you do, whether in word or deed, do it all in the name of the Lord Jesus.

—Colossians 3:17

Mom
I Love You!

$\mathcal{T}$he beauty of the house is order;
  The blessing of the house is contentment;
  The glory of the house is hospitality;
  The crown of the house is godliness.

—Fireplace motto

Mom
I Love You!

$\mathcal{T}$hose who sow in tears
will reap with songs of joy.

—*Psalm 126:5*

Mom
I Love You!

Christ be with me, Christ be within me
Christ beside me, Christ to win me
Christ to comfort and restore me
Christ beneath me, Christ above me
Christ in quiet, Christ in danger
Christ in hearts of all that love me
Christ in friend and stranger

❧

—*Prayer of St. Patrick*

$\mathcal{L}$ove is patient, love is kind.

❧

—*1 Corinthians 13:4*

Mom
I Love You!

$\mathcal{S}$trength of character may be acquired
at work, but beauty of character is learned
at home. There the affections are trained.
There the gentle life reaches us, the true
heaven life. In one word, the family circle
is the supreme conductor of Christianity.

—Henry Drummond

Mom
I Love You!

The LORD'S unfailing
love surrounds the man
who trusts in him.

❧

—*Psalm 32:10*

Mom
I Love You!

$\mathscr{F}$ remember my mother's prayers
and they have always followed me.
They have clung to me all my life.

—*Abraham Lincoln*

Mom
I Love You!

Set your hope fully on the
grace to be given you when
Jesus Christ is revealed.

—1 Peter 1:13

Mom

I Love You!

When one door of happiness
closes, another opens.

—*Helen Keller*

Mom
I Love You!

Create in me a pure heart, O God,
and renew a steadfast spirit within
me. . . .
Restore to me the joy of your salvation
and grant me a willing spirit, to
sustain me.

—Psalm 51:10,12

Mom

I Love You!

$\mathcal{T}$he woman who creates and sustains a home, and under whose hands children grow up to be strong and pure men and women, is a creator second only to God.

—Helen Hunt Jackson

Mom

I Love You!

$\mathcal{W}$ho of you by worrying can
add a single hour to his life?

—*Matthew 6:27*

Mom I Love You!

$\mathcal{A}$re your children grown? Yet in
your mind they are still your little
ones, so bring those grown men or
women to Jesus as the children
you know them to be. Jesus will
touch them and bless them.

❧

—*Rosalind Rinker*

Mom
I Love You!

Consider how the lilies grow. They do not labor or spin. Yet I tell you, not even Solomon in all his splendor was dressed like one of these. If that is how God clothes the grass of the field . . . how much more will he clothe you.

—*Luke 12:27–28*

Mom

I Love You!

$\mathcal{Y}$et in the maddening maze of things,
And tossed by storm and flood,
To one fixed trust my spirit clings;
I know that God is good!

—John Greenleaf Whittier

Mom

I Love You!

$\mathcal{B}$efore they call I will answer;
while they are still speaking I
will hear.

❧

—*Isaiah 65:24*

Mom

I Love You!

$\mathcal{L}$ord, behold our family here assembled.
We thank Thee for this place in which we
dwell; for the love that unites us; for the
peace accorded to us this day, for the
health, the work, the food, and the bright
skies that make our lives delightful.

❧

—Robert Louis Stevenson

111

"*M*any women do noble things,
but you surpass them all."

—*Proverbs 31:29*

Mom

I Love You!

$\mathcal{N}$o gold or jeweled gift can
crown a mother's life like a
simple word of gratitude
from her beloved child.

✂

—*Pat Matuszak*

Mom

I Love You!

$\mathcal{L}$et us hold unswervingly to
the hope we profess, for he
who promised is faithful.

❧

—*Hebrews 10:23*

Mom
I Love You!

$\mathcal{W}$e entered motherhood so
eagerly—babes in our arms
and stars in our eyes. So cuddly
and cute, these wee ones took
hold of our hearts and lives.

❧

—*Diane Head*

115

Mom
I Love You!

$\mathcal{L}$et your conversation
be always full of grace.

❧

—Colossians 4:6

Mom

I Love You!

$\mathcal{T}$hy love is such I can no way repay;
The heavens reward thee manifold, I pray.

—*Anne Bradstreet*

Mom
I Love You!

*F*t is the LORD's
purpose that prevails.

—*Proverbs 19:21*

Mom
I Love You!

$\mathcal{D}$are to dream. Help our
children dream. Reach out and
take the dream God has for you.

❧

—*Wintley Phipps*

Mom

I Love You!

$\mathcal{D}$o not forget the things your
eyes have seen or let them slip
from your heart as long as you
live. Teach them to your children
and to their children after them.

❧

—*Deuteronomy 4:9*

Mom

I Love You!

The things we do today—sowing seeds, or sharing simple truths of Christ—people will someday refer to as the first things that prompted them to think of him.

❦

—George Matheson

Mom
I Love You!

$\mathcal{M}$ay she who gave
you birth rejoice!

—*Proverbs 23:25*

*M*other's arms under you,
Her eyes above you
Sing it high, sing it low,
Love me—I love you.

—Christina Rossetti

Mom
I Love You!

*T*he Lord has made everything
beautiful in its time.

—Ecclesiastes 3:11

Mom

I Love You!

$\mathcal{D}$on't aim to be an earthly saint
with eyes fixed on a star:
Just try to be the person that your
mother thinks you are.

❧

—*Will S. Adkin*

$\mathcal{L}$et the peace of Christ rule in
your hearts. . . . And be thankful.

❧

—*Colossians 3:15*

Mom
I Love You!

$\mathscr{T}$he greater part of our
happiness or misery depends
on our dispositions, and
not on our circumstances.

❧

—*Martha Washington*

Sources

Selections From
The Women's Devotional Bible 2.
Grand Rapids: Zondervan, 1995.
God's Wisdom for Women Daybreak.
Grand Rapids: Zondervan, 1996.
Blessings of a Mother's Love
Grand Rapids: Zondervan, 1999.